Cornerstones of Freedom

Mount Vernon

MARY COLLINS

CHILDREN'S PRESS®
A Division of Grolier Publishing
New York • London • Hong Kong • Sydney
Danbury, Connecticut

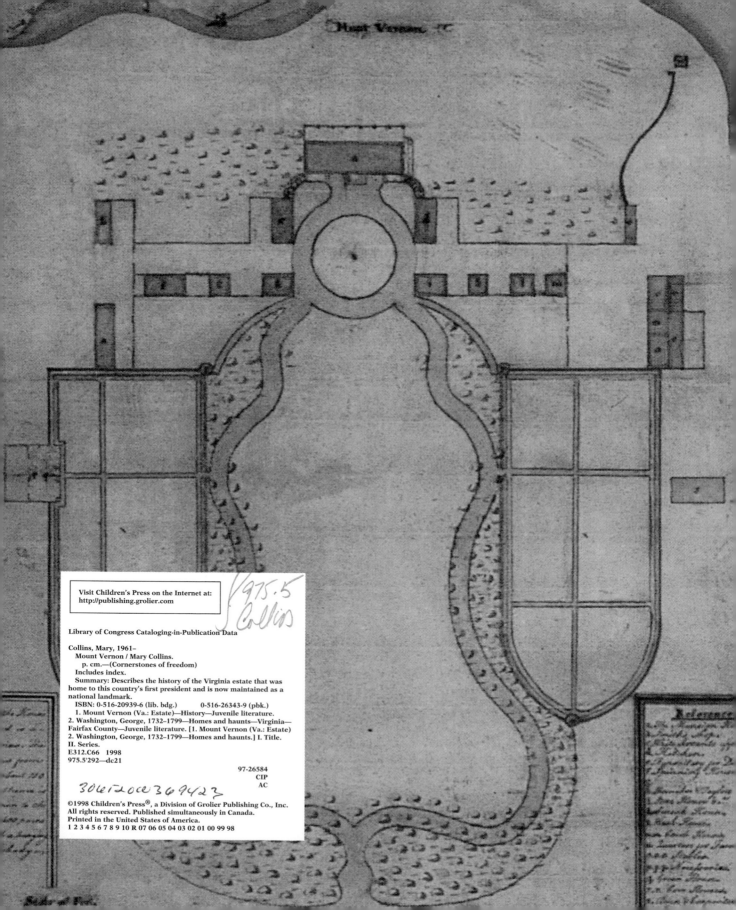

Library of Congress Cataloging-in-Publication Data

Collins, Mary, 1961–
    Mount Vernon / Mary Collins.
        p. cm.—(Cornerstones of freedom)
    Includes index.
    Summary: Describes the history of the Virginia estate that was
home to this country's first president and is now maintained as a
national landmark.
    ISBN: 0-516-20939-6 (lib. bdg.)   0-516-26343-9 (pbk.)
    1. Mount Vernon (Va.: Estate)—History—Juvenile literature.
2. Washington, George, 1732–1799—Homes and haunts—Virginia—
Fairfax County—Juvenile literature. [1. Mount Vernon (Va.: Estate)
2. Washington, George, 1732–1799—Homes and haunts.] I. Title.
II. Series.
E312.C66   1998
975.5'292—dc21
                                                        97-26584
                                                             CIP
                                                             AC

30612002369423

Hundreds of years before George Washington (1732–99) made Mount Vernon his home, an Algonquian Indian tribe roamed the glorious hill on the land that overlooks the Potomac River. They left behind bones, pottery, and other evidence of their passing. Several generations of English settlers farmed the fields. By the time Washington inherited the property in 1761, countless Indians, trappers, fishermen, farmers, and explorers had already crossed through its forests and fields many times. He was clearly not the only man to make his home there.

American Indians were the first people to live in the area that is now Mount Vernon.

George Washington

George Washington's home sits high on a bluff overlooking the Potomac River.

But today we value George Washington's Virginia plantation, located just a few miles south of Washington, D.C., because he lived there. As commander in chief of the Continental Army, he led the rebellion against the British during the Revolutionary War (1775–83). As the first president, he served from 1789 to 1797 and helped to shape our new government. He played such an important role in making our country what it is today that millions of people travel to his estate at Mount Vernon to learn more about the public and private life of this Founding Father.

"No estate in United America is more pleasantly situated than this [Mount Vernon]," Washington wrote in a letter in 1793. "It lies in a high, dry, and healthy country, three hundred miles [483 kilometers] by water from the sea, and . . . on one of the finest rivers in the world." The general loved his home and returned to it whenever he could. But his public duties as a soldier and politician kept him so busy that he once went eight years with no more than a day's visit home.

The mansion's location offers a spectacular view of the Potomac River and the hills of Maryland.

The nation's capital as we know it today was just a mosquito-infested swamp during Washington's time. The new government held most of its meetings in Philadelphia or New York City. There were no trains, paved roads, cars, or airplanes then, so travelers had to work their way over muddy roads on horseback. A journey from Mount Vernon to New York, a distance of about 250 miles (402 km), could take weeks, which helps explain why Washington did not return home as often as he would have liked.

Before the war, Washington made some major additions to the modest, one-level house he inherited. When he married the widow Martha Dandridge Custis in 1759, he added a second floor to make room for his new wife and her two young children. Most of the other big renovations, including the large dining room where Washington loved to dance, were not completed until after the war. Work was slow. One room took twelve years to finish because the workers had to import most of the materials, such as the sparkling powders they mixed with oil, turpentine, and arsenic to make paint. The plaster ceiling alone required months of messy work.

"I have scarcely a room to put a friend into or to set in myself without the music of hammers or the [odorous] smell of paint," Washington remarked in a letter to a friend in 1797. Carpenters, plasterers, and painters worked for years to finish the house as visitors see it today.

While serving as commander in chief of the Continental Army, General Washington directed the building and decoration of the large dining room through letters.

The wide lawn leading up to the mansion looks today much as it did in Washington's time.

Washington was most content when he spent time at Mount Vernon with his wife, Martha, and his stepchildren, John and Martha.

Washington himself only enjoyed the long, wide lawn leading up to his house in the final years of his life, because it simply wasn't finished before then. He carefully selected and planted rows of trees along the carriage drive. Some of these original saplings still stand today, though they are now spectacular trees fat with old age.

After all his glory in battle, after serving eight years as our country's first president, Washington still felt his happiest days were spent at Mount Vernon with his family, friends,

and fields. "I can truly say I had rather be at home at Mount Vernon with a friend or two about me than to be attended at the seat of government by the officers of states and the representatives of every power in Europe," he wrote in 1790. Most history books focus on Washington as a soldier and president, but Washington considered himself first and foremost a farmer. He loved to ride through his fields and forests and along the banks of the wide Potomac River.

George Washington enjoyed touring the grounds of his plantation.

Washington made this record of his slaves and their occupations in 1799 as part of his will, which provided for some of them to be released upon his death.

When Washington first became master of Mount Vernon, the plantation included fewer than fifty slaves, a few simple buildings, and some tobacco fields. By the end of his life, more than three hundred slaves worked the five farms that made up his 8,000-acre (3,237-hectare) plantation (six times more land than what we see today at the estate). Like many of the leading men in colonial America, Washington was deeply conflicted about the issue of owning slaves. When he died, his will directed that several of his slaves would be freed (most notably his personal servant William Lee, who served with him during the Revolutionary War). But Washington did not free them all. While he lived, Washington never resolved the conflict within himself regarding the right of any man to "own" another. Martha, however, freed Washington's remaining slaves (about 105 of them) a year after her husband's death.

Only Washington's sense of duty drew him away from Mount Vernon into the stressful life of a field general and political figure. If his primary concern had been his own happiness, he probably would have remained at his haven most of his adult life. Instead, he endured the great discomforts of the battlefield and the strains of the presidency for the sake of a more noble goal: freedom from the tyranny of English rule.

George Washington's bedroom, including the bed in which he died on December 14, 1799

On those peaceful days when he was at home, he awoke before sunrise and descended the narrow staircase between his bedroom and study. The washstand and mirror that he used for shaving still sits pressed against the far wall. He ate breakfast at 7:00 A.M., preferring three Indian hoe cakes (similar to pancakes) "swimming in butter and honey" and three cups of tea.

Make Your Own Hoe Cakes

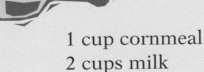

1 cup cornmeal
2 cups milk
1/2 teaspoon salt

2 beaten eggs
1 cup flour
4 tablespoons honey

Mix together the cornmeal, flour, and salt. Heat the milk until it just begins to boil (steam appears). Pour it into the dry mixture. Add the honey and eggs. Stir just until the ingredients are wet. Spoon batter onto a hot, oiled griddle. Turn to brown both sides.

SOURCE: *Mount Vernon Hands-on History*, Mount Vernon Ladies' Association, ©1996, p. 44.

Some days he would ride around his estate, and other days he might experiment with new plants in what he liked to call his "little garden." The garden still exists today much as Washington kept it. During his forty-five years as master of Mount Vernon, he tried out sixty plant varieties in his fields. He sent away for seeds from some of the finest farmers in America and England, and he constantly worked at getting the most out of his lands. Early on Washington switched from Virginia's most popular crop, tobacco, to wheat, potatoes, corn, and oats. He believed the tobacco took too much from the soil, and the land quickly lost its fertility.

Washington's garden, in which he experimented with several plant varieties

Washington became expert at crop rotation, which involves knowing what to plant, when, and for how long. Sometimes certain fields had to lie fallow—which means nothing was grown on them except perhaps grass or clover—so they could regain the rich nutrients that crops need to grow well. The general also designed a remarkable sixteen-sided barn made of brick and wood. It allowed the workers to thrash the wheat inside using horses that walked on the stalks. (This was different from the more traditional method of having slaves thrash wheat by hand outside with big sticks.) The most edible portions of the wheat or grain would fall through the cracks in the floor to the hold below. This clean area protected the grain from rain, insects, and dirt.

The sixteen-sided barn has been restored to look much the way it did when Washington designed it.

Today summertime visitors to Mount Vernon can stop by a re-creation of the famous barn and watch volunteers harvest the wheat and other crops much as field hands did during Washington's day. Hoes with long wooden handles lie against the exposed dirt. Two horses go round and round as they crack the stalks in the July heat.

Visitors to the barn can watch horses thrash the wheat to separate the grain from the stalk.

The sixteen-sided barn overlooks the Potomac River, where Washington had a successful fishery. Before pollution and over-fishing destroyed much of the wildlife in the capital area, the river brimmed with life. Sturgeons that could live for a hundred years and grow more than 12 feet (4 meters) long joined the huge runs of shad and bass. In one year, Washington's workers hauled in a million fish!

When the British explorer John Smith first traveled to this part of the river in 1608, he found "such an abundance of fish, lying quite thick, with their heads above the water, as our barge drove through them, that for want of a net we attempted to catch them with a frying-pan." Today, thanks to clean-up and conservation efforts, some of the fish are returning, but the river has a long way to go before it returns to the bounty of Washington's time.

Mount Vernon functioned like a little village, complete with blacksmith, shoemaker, baker, and more. Washington was hardly the only person who awoke at the break of day. "The sun never caught George Washington in bed and he was unwilling to find any of his people sleeping," one former slave recalled in 1838. They had too much to do!

In addition to the hundreds of people who lived and worked the plantation, as many as four hundred guests stopped by in a year. They

Captain John Smith was one of the settlers of Jamestown, Virginia, the first permanent English settlement in North America.

The buildings and "roads" of Mount Vernon made it look more like a village than a plantation.

came from all over the world to see the United States's famous general. The common courtesy of the day called for them to be provided with food and a bed, even if they were uninvited strangers. The Washingtons did their best to accommodate the crowds. In one letter to a friend, the general compared Mount Vernon to "a well-resorted tavern as scarcely any strangers who are going from north to south or from south to north do not spend a day or two at it."

Upon arrival at Mount Vernon, visitors entered the mansion's main hall.

While George and Martha must have found entertaining all those guests an exhausting task, the slaves who prepared all the food and beds worked even harder. Simple chores that are done so easily today, such as laundry, involved hours of tedious labor.

Dolly and Sall, two washerwomen at Mount Vernon, could not simply gather all the dirty things and toss them into a machine with some detergent because there was neither electricity nor supermarkets. First they had to make big

The laundry house in which women, such as Dolly and Sall, worked six days a week

Laundry was hung out to dry in the yard behind the laundry house.

bricks of soap from animal fat and lye (which is made by pouring boiling water through wood ashes). Then they sent some of the slave children off to gather water from the well in buckets that weighed up to 25 pounds (11 kilograms) when full. When the big copper or brass kettles were full of water, soap, and dirty laundry, the women went to work pounding the laundry and stirring it with long poles. They rinsed the clean items several times, then hung them out to dry. On the days when it rained, they had to build a big fire inside the laundry house and hang everything up. But that's not the end of it. They still had to starch, iron, and put away all the items. After eight to ten hours of this hard labor, they had to wake up the next day and start all over again—six days a week.

Food preparation required just as much work. Martha Washington planned the menus and oversaw the preparation of most meals, but the slave help, such as Old Doll and Hercules, did the rolling, mixing, and baking. Just to make the general's breakfast they had to first milk the cow, churn the butter, collect firewood and start a fire, gather eggs, and grind and measure the Indian corn meal. They had to get up mighty early to make sure they had his breakfast cooked by 7:00 A.M.!

Other buildings on the plantation included the smokehouse, where men cut up pigs and other sources of meat. The meat was then smoked and salted so it wouldn't spoil (remember, refrigerators had not yet been invented). At the blacksmith's shop, every nail, horseshoe, and other metal items had to be forged by hand. In another building, the shoemaker could make or repair as many as four hundred pairs of shoes in a year. Elsewhere, the cooper made the wooden barrels and buckets that stored everything from potatoes to water. And in the spinning room, linen and wool were spun into thread and yarn.

Modern reenactors demonstrate the work of Washington's blacksmiths.

Older women or new mothers recovering from their pregnancies made up some of the work force in the spinning room. There, a plant called flax was broken down into fibers and spun into thread. The women also took the wool gathered from the many sheep that roamed the plantation (as many as one thousand) and spun it into yarn. Weak slaves who could not work in the fields could sit at the spinning wheels or run combs, also called "carding," through the wool. They made most of the clothes worn by the slaves at Mount Vernon.

During the Revolutionary War, Washington urged his cousin Lund Washington, who was supervising the estate in the general's absence, to make sure that "Spinning go forward with [great speed] for we shall have nothing else to depend upon if these disputes (war with England) continue." Both soldiers and slaves alike prized the limited supply of clothes they received. On the plantation, each male slave was given one pair of pants, two shirts, some stockings (which are similar to thick leggings), and a pair of shoes—for the year. The general and his family had a larger, fancier wardrobe, which included imported materials such as silk, fine buttons, and cotton. But even the Washingtons got by with far fewer clothes than the average person wears today.

Many of the slaves lived in small cabins near the fields where most of them worked. Others, however, lived in a cramped room just off to the side of the main house called The Greenhouse Slave Quarters. It was no bigger than today's average living room. A dozen bunk beds lined the walls. A crude wooden table was the only thing that broke up the long room, which had a large fireplace at one end for cooking and heat. One family that lived in this confined space included Isaac the carpenter, his wife Kitty, and their nine daughters.

Although the original slave quarters was destroyed by fire in 1835, the reconstructed building closely resembles Washington's design.

By the mid-1800s, Mount Vernon barely resembled George Washington's beautiful plantation.

Mount Vernon now stands as an active, vibrant example of eighteenth-century Virginia plantation life because some concerned southern women refused to let it slip into ruin. The place tourists visit today, with its shining lawn, blooming gardens, and well-cared-for

buildings, lay in complete disrepair by the mid-1800s. "All is shabby as possible," a French visitor wrote in 1840. "The park is grown over with weeds; the house tumbling down; everything dirty and in a miserable condition."

John Augustine Washington Jr., the last of a series of family owners, found it impossible to maintain Mount Vernon and deal with the endless stream of visitors who regarded the site as a sacred national shrine. He offered to sell the house and 200 acres (81 hectares) to the federal government for $200,000, which was a fair price. Congress, however, would not give him the money. A private businessman who wanted to make it into a tourist attraction similar to an amusement park offered John Washington $300,000, but he declined. Washington understood that Mount Vernon was a place that people held in great respect. It was hardly the spot for a crude, money-making opportunity.

John A. Washington Jr., great-grandnephew of George Washington

Ann Pamela Cunningham (fourth from right) organized the Mount Vernon Ladies' Association.

John had given up hope of saving the property when Ann Pamela Cunningham of South Carolina appeared on the scene. She had been running ads in southern newspapers, urging women to help her raise money to save General Washington's home. They answered her plea and raised enough money to offer John Washington $200,000 for the house and land. The Mount Vernon Ladies' Association (MVLA) continues to run the estate today. It has worked furiously over the years to rebuild the sagging house, add more land to the estate, and regain many of the personal objects that Washington owned, such as the swivel chair in his study, which he used during his presidency.

The swivel chair in Washington's study is the same one in which he sat while serving as the first president of the United States.

The MVLA set a great example for all the preservation organizations that have followed them since. They have gone to great lengths to make sure that present-day visitors see an authentic representation of what was in the house in 1799. Authentic means that something looks as it actually did, not as we expect or want it to look. For example, when workers repainted the large dining room to match the color Washington chose, they used the same recipe for the paint—powder, oil, turpentine, and arsenic—and the same French round brushes. The result: The color on the walls often looks uneven and has an unusual oily

The distinctive paint color used for the dining room was meticulously reproduced using samples of the original.

shine to it that we don't see in the paints we use in our homes today. What matters is that it looks the way Washington would have seen it.

When Ann Cunningham resigned as head of the Mount Vernon Ladies' Association, she told her fellow volunteers: "Those who go to the home in which [Washington] lived and died wish to see in what he lived and died. Let one spot in this grand country of ours be saved from change." Thanks to the efforts of private citizens like Ann, Mount Vernon does look much as Washington left it at the time of his death.

More than one million people visit Mount Vernon each year.

In 1784, the Revolutionary War had ended and Washington believed he had finally returned to his treasured Mount Vernon for good. Of course, today we know he went on to serve as the first president of the United States. But at the time he wrote the following letter to a fellow soldier, he thought his public duties had ended:

"At length I am become a private citizen on the banks of the Potomac, and under the shadow

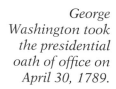

George Washington took the presidential oath of office on April 30, 1789.

of my own Vine and my own Fig-tree, free from the bustle of camp and the busy scenes of public life, I am solacing myself with . . . tranquil enjoyments . . . I am not only retired from public enjoyments, but I am retiring within myself; and shall be able to view the solitary walk, and tread the paths of private life with heartfelt satisfaction. Envious of none, I am determined to be pleased with all; and this my friend, being the order for my march, I will move gently down the stream of life, until I sleep with my Fathers."

In 1799, George Washington died at his beloved home at the age of sixty-seven. Today at Mount Vernon, Americans can still peer into the private world of a man who did so much to make our country the free, independent nation it is today.

George Washington is buried on the grounds of Mount Vernon. The stone tablet above the entrance to his tomb reads, "Within this Enclosure Rest the remains of [General] George Washington."

GLOSSARY

conservation – careful use of wild plants, animals, fish, and birds to prevent their exploitation or extinction

crop rotation – switching crops in a field because each plant affects the soil differently

crude – rude, or in poor taste

fishery – place where fish are bred

forge – to make or to form

haven – safe place

imported – product that comes from a foreign country

national shrine

national shrine – place that is loved and respected because of events or people associated with it

plaster – wet substance made from sand, lime, clay, and hair that filled in the space between the wooden slats in an indoor wall; after drying, it could be painted

preservation – protecting something so that it stays in its original state

renovations – work that restores something to good condition, or makes it more modern

thrash

starch – to add a white substance to cloth to make it stiff

thrash – to beat crops to separate the seeds from the husks and straw

tyranny – cruel or unjust rule over a nation or its people

TIMELINE

1732 *February 22:* George Washington born

Lawrence Washington dies; his wife inherits Mount Vernon **1752**

1754 Lawrence's widow moves away from Mount Vernon; George leases the estate

George Washington marries Martha Dandridge Custis **1759**

1761 George Washington inherits Mount Vernon

1775 Revolutionary War begins; Washington commands Continental Army

Revolutionary War ends; Washington retires to Mount Vernon **1783**

George Washington serves as first president of the United States { **1789**

1797

1799

December 14: George Washington dies

May 22: Martha Washington dies **1802**

MVLA purchases Mount Vernon; restoration begins

1829 John A. Washington inherits Mount Vernon

1858

1861 }

1865 } American Civil War; Northern and Southern commanders agree not to fight on Mount Vernon

INDEX (*Boldface* page numbers indicate illustrations.)

PHOTO CREDITS

Photographs ©: Andrew H. MacDonald: 1, 4 bottom, 5, 12, 13, 15, 17, 27, 30; AP/Wide World Photos: 4 top; Cameramann Int'l Ltd.: cover; Mount Vernon Ladies Association: 2, 6 bottom, 7, 8 top, 10, 11, 15 bottom, 16, 18, 21, 22, 23, 24, 25, 26, 28, 29, 31; North Wind Picture Archives: 3, 6 top, 8 bottom, 9, 14; ZEFA/H.Armstrong Roberts: 19.

ABOUT THE AUTHOR

Mary Collins lives in Alexandria, Virginia, and teaches writing at the graduate level at Johns Hopkins University. She is also a freelance writer whose work includes articles for newspapers, magazines, and a medical encyclopedia. Ms. Collins has published several books on a variety of subjects for companies such as Time-Life. Ms. Collins is the author of *The Spanish-American War* (Cornerstones of Freedom) for Children's Press.